Efflorescence

poems by

Dawn Marar

Finishing Line Press
Georgetown, Kentucky

Efflorescence

for
Hani George,
Lauren Elizabeth, and Petra Helena

Copyright © 2018 by Dawn Marar
ISBN 978-1-63534-446-2 First Edition
All rights reserved under International and Pan-American Copyright Conventions. No part of this book may be reproduced in any manner whatsoever without written permission from the publisher, except in the case of brief quotations embodied in critical articles and reviews.

ACKNOWLEDGMENTS

"Efflorescence," *Chautauqua Literary Journal, contest finalist.*
"American Sampler of Arabic Vocabulary," *Jelly Bucket for Reading, creative nonfiction. Nominated for the Pushcart Prize.*
"Manna from Heaven," *Orison Anthology Awards for Poetry, finalist.*
"Cross Border," *36 Views Of Ononta'kahrhon, BlogSpot. Haibun-photo collaborative project with Mark W. O'Brien.*
"Manna from Heaven," "On the Road to Damascus," and "Mayday Mayday Mayday," *Nimrod International Journal of Prose and Poetry. These poems received The Nimrod Literary Awards, The Pablo Neruda Prize for Poetry, finalist.*

Special thank you to the Evergreen Poets Workshop

Publisher: Leah Maines
Editor: Christen Kincaid
Cover Art: Dawn Marar
Author Photo: Hani G. Marar
Cover Design: Elizabeth Maines McCleavy

Printed in the USA on acid-free paper.
Order online: www.finishinglinepress.com
also available on amazon.com

Author inquiries and mail orders:
Finishing Line Press
P. O. Box 1626
Georgetown, Kentucky 40324
U. S. A.

Table of Contents

Sparkles 1

Working Out 2

Mayday Mayday Mayday 3

A.E.I.O.U. 5

American Sampler of Arabic Vocabulary 6

Lowly and Happy Bitterness 7

Manna from Heaven 9

Sea Creature 11

A Story of Biblical Proportions 12

On the Road to Damascus 13

A Bit of Mercy 14

Dispatch from Beit Jala, near Bethlehem 15

Baptism—Al-Maghtas المغطس 16

Basilica Cistern 18

Gadarene Rush 19

Snowomen 20

Fusion Approach to Gathering 21

Efflorescence 22

Heavenly Bodies 25

Cue the Leaf Blower 27

Endgame 28

Agora 29

Cross Border 30

Notes 31

And after efflorescence,—decay; the old organization, by degrees, dissolved in the greater freedom of art.

Sparkles

In the Sixties, two teens—five thousand miles/nine thousand kilometers apart—listened to songs of summer: the girl on a transistor radio in a village named Green Island to Scott McKenzie's "San Francisco (Be Sure to Wear Flowers in Your Hair)," and the boy on a shortwave radio in Baghdad to Fairuz' "Al-Quds Ya Zahrat Al-Madayn (Jerusalem: the Flower of Cities)." When it rained, the tar-papered roof in the wood shack where the girl lived leaked. Even laundry hung inside to dry got wet. Despite rain, no grass grew in the backyard. It never rained in Baghdad in summer, so the boy often slept on the rooftop. And yet, there was a grassy yard. Down the street from the brick house where the boy lived, the party in power hung its enemies in Tahrir Square. The girl dreamed of Jerusalem; the boy, of America. As adults they met at Sparkles, a disco—not far from where the girl grew up and where the boy became a hospital fellow. They raised two daughters in Bethlehem; one now lives in the US capital and the other in San Francisco.

<blockquote>
A fig tree housed
in winter bears fruit, despite
a new world order.
</blockquote>

Working Out

Cruising into the parking lot, on the radio I heard, "The American
government, now in Istanbul and in Amman, is shopping
among former Iraqi generals and tribal sheikhs asking,
Who is willing to come and fight the Islamic State?"

I gripped the wheel, focusing on the open space ahead.
In the next row, a man slams the trunk of his SUV. Come spring
my husband and I will travel to the Middle East—
shop for kilims in Istanbul and visit family in Amman.

The beepbeepbeep of a construction vehicle backing up
echoed. "Jordan is safe," Hani said this morning. I am not so sure.
His sister and niece have been granted Canadian visas.
But the young woman refuses to emigrate, despite job
 opportunities. Neither does Aida really want to leave.

I turned off the radio, cut the engine. Wind rustled tree tops at the edge
 of the parking lot. Inside, women worked out in Forever Fit,
Deep Water Workout, and Latin Rhythms Boot Camp.
Inside EMTs, night shift troopers, police, and firefighters lifted
heavy weights, ran legion on treadmills. Retired vets pumped lighter iron.

Through tears, winged sumac, scarlet oak, sugar maple leaves burst into
 flames.
A train whistle signaled the arrival of North Dakota crude.
I was surrounded by Toyotas, Hundai, Chevies, BMWs, Mercedes Benz.
A truck coasted downhill. Lining the entrance to the gym, red mums.

Once inside a rumbling up around the corner turned out to be just
a clean-up trolley. I worked out alone. I practiced squats
should my husband and I visit some remote location
where I'll need strong glutes, hamstrings, quads, and *erector spinae*.

Mayday Mayday Mayday

5...
In prep for take-off I visit my defunct Twitter feed,
check on Turkey, and find the President
shut down social media. Erdoğan is afraid
of a little bird. The hotel let us know that
when we arrive we'd see security forces
in strategic locations. We were asked to "kindly be vigilant
for [our] own comfort." They offered to pick us up
at Ataturk Airport with a Mercedes Sprinter.
In our best most arrogant ignorant American selves
my husband and I joked about intrigue;
clinked another round of *rakı*.
4...
Taksim Square, Istanbul. Erdoğan's vision:
a security lockdown—for the First of May
"to be celebrated in a festive mood without provocations."
Shuttered shops and metal barricades stand in
for humane leadership. Recep Tayyip stages
a B grade movie scene: helicopters swoop swarm.
Metro stations close, as does the funicular
to the ferry; intercity Bosphorous bus runs
on limited schedules. 25,000 *polis* stationed
about the Square earn their pay as @RT_Erdoğan
hides out 453 kilometers away
in Ak Saray, the White Palace in Ankara.
3...
The Reservation Agent was wrong.
The Sprinter had no special permission to cross police
roadblocks. So Hani and I get out and hoof
the empty streets to the hotel.

2...
Later we leave the hotel to go out a walkin past
officers riot gear plexiglass shields helmets guns
busloads of reserves, some dozing.
Passersby couples old men children
as if extras on a set waiting for a shoot.
We reach the Square barriers and Hani spies
his favorite dish in a *Self-servis*
restaurant window: *domatesli bamya*.
Inside we sit among locals and reinforcements eating kepabs.
I sneak upstairs snap pictures out the window.

Back at the hotel this time we see footage
of the other side of the Square treated
to tear gas rubber bullets armored vehicles water cannons.

1...
That night in Istanbul we watched
on CNN the curfew in the States
where it had been no holiday. In Baltimore,
1,000 marchers protested the death
of Freddie Gray following injuries
sustained in police custody. For days,
2,000 National Guardsmen, 1,000+ police
officers used pepper balls and smoke grenades
enforcing a state of emergency.

A.E.I.O.U.

English
Speakers might be tempted
To finish the phrase
                  and sometimes
                              Y
Go against the initial
Instinct
To toss it
Offhandedly
      History demands
We, as Americans,
                              fathom the why
                  that may not be
                  self-evident
We hold
These
                              Remember that
                              All people are

American Sampler of Arabic Vocabulary

These days we speak of Baghdad's *occupation*.   استحلال
It might not seem unusual to ask for a *female/male*
   translator, but that strikes me as awfully formal, even in a   مترجم\
   Middle Eastern family.   مترجمة
No one in my husband Hani's family is in the *army*.   جيش
Hence, it follows that there is/are no *officer/officers* either.   ضابط\ضباط
I am always saying, *Let's go!* to the Dead Sea or Petra or
   Mount Nebo.   يلا بنا
I might only *search* for the perfect souvenir to bring back to
   the States.   بحث
On occasion, I discuss one's *[political] party* or *wars*.   حزب حروب
But *shrapnel*? *Evacuation*?   شظية خلاء
I suppose *coughing*, but *shame*?   سعال عيب
Maybe I could ask if someone's condition is *painful*, or,
   what are your fondest memories of *Baghdad*?   اليم بغداد
His family has never held anyone *captive*.   اسير
I would rather not speak with family about the *oppressor*.   طاغي
I never saw a *riot* in Jordan, although I heard about
   demonstrations in Kerak when the price of pita got too high.   شغب
We usually speak of the Palestinian Territories, which, of
   course, includes *Gaza*.   غزة
Why are students taught to say *he swallowed (something)/it*?   بلع
We always know what the "something," or the "it" is. It is no
   mystery.
Why would I be taught to say *he is making it complicated*?   يعقد
Iran—we don't talk much about.   ايران
If something is overcooked, we would not speak of it as   احرق
   burned.
How would I use the phrase *take down building*?   هدم
No one ever goes *barefoot*.   حافي
One always wishes *peace*.   سلام
Only if I had traveler's sickness would I say *I have pain*.   عندي الم
Whenever I have been in Jordan, there has never been an
   emergency nor a *revolution*.   طوارىء\ثورة
But I suppose that's not to say it couldn't happen.

Lowly and Happy Bitterness

I paced
       like the fox
              that I am
my red fur—hair—catching
the glint of the brass shop lamp
in my reflection
Now every Arab would know
              I am low lowly
              I am poor inferior
              I am meager
              I am inadequate   as my husband spelled
in Arabic the literal transcription of the phonetic pronunciation
of my given name, Dawn
                    daal waaw noon
                                        دون
                              (pronounced
              in Arabic) doon, which means low
                lowly poor inferior meager inadequate
                    (The Arabic word for dawn
                                فجر
            fajir is rarely if ever used as a first name)

What kind of an Arabian—man—marries a woman who is known
as Lowlowlypoorinferiormeagerinadequate
I paced along the wall from which Christ
carved in native olive wood hung beside Koranic verses
on bright ceramic plates as Youssef
 the jeweler from Jerusalem drilled
the letters for a sterling silver pendant

Must I wear upon my scarlet décolletage
such an avowal
My husband told Youssef our surname   Marar
                                                                      مرار
                                                          which means bitter

What kind of an Arab marries a woman who is known to be Inadequate and makes her Bitter

                                            The kind who is named Hani

                                                                  هاني

                                              which means happy

Manna from Heaven

We were lucky to be in Amman soon after Easter
when Hani's brother served من السما —*mann ilsama*—manna from
  Heaven.

Some speculate Moses' manna was really magic mushrooms.
The *mann ilsama* in Jordan today—not far from where Moses

led his people near the King's Highway—
is made in Iraq. And only at this time of year.

Today Iraq's manna comes from tamarisk tree resin.
I removed the waxed paper wrapper and a dusting of flour fell

upon my white pants. I bit into the lumpy rock gingerly
releasing a taste of cardamon laced with pistachios.

Decades ago—at home in the States—I tried magic
mushrooms but the Hudson River did not part.

Nor did anyone lead people out of the village of Green Island
to the promised land of Troy. Yet over the years I had

other visions. When I travel to the Middle East
I am vigilant. Vision in Jordan was thwarted on this trip

by the خماسين—*khamasin* winds—which arrived from the Atlas
  Mountains
in North Africa. Dust kicked up so thick I wore a blue surgical mask.

Not long before I left, I treated my niece to bubblegum
flavored tobacco to smoke in a hookah on the balcony.

Then I settled inside to read the newspaper
where I learned about a man in Syria. Ordnance rained

from heaven in the Douma neighborhood of Damascus.
Abu Khalid, using remnants of weapons, rockets

and tank shells, rolled out the dough to make barley
bread which his son then sold on the street.

Sea Creature

Atop Mount Nebo above the Dead
Sea, I entered the Memorial
Church of Moses, finding this fossilized
creature, for a nominal fee, among Holy
Land incense and myrrh. Ancient Mediterranean
ancestor, I carried across Europe and the Atlantic.

Home in the New World, my gaze falls
upon the petrified heart-shaped sea creature
whom I do and do not want to embrace.
I set you down, and you rest, tilted,
pointed like Brancusi's *Sleeping Muse.*

Like a sweet black cherry pit with a Rock
Hudson cleft chin. Bone tint and hint
of bewildered orbital socket. Timidly I roll
you over and I'm smitten, buff sparrow. Skull
and streamlined wing above a bright breast.

Turning you over again I see the strong brow
of the eagle, compressed millions of years.
Grumpy hooked beak and eye closed. At turns
delicate and stern. My thumb pushes
against Nature's grit and you pivot.

Now, netsuke-like: a fawn draped over a rock,
ears pinned back. Or a fox. Or again the bald
eagle's head worn smooth by desert winds.
What would you say if you could, old sea being.

A Story of Biblical Proportions

I dipped an empty plastic water bottle
labeled *Hayat* —الحياة— into the man-made baptismal
pool at Bethany Beyond the Jordan.
Hayat means "life." Unlike the Jordan River
that day, the water looked clear.
But I knew it was not potable.
So, I wrote in permanent
marker: *Do Not Drink*.

Years later at home I found the bottle
in the basement. It still contained water,
although, it was warped—
as if the life had been sucked
out of it. Something stirred
on the bottom as I lifted it. An emerald
gobbet I'd not seen before—amoeba-surreal—
encased in a filmy viscous substance.

I didn't want to destroy—to break up—
this artifact of feeble pilgrimage.

The bottle's rippled design magnified
the distortion. Was that an eye?
A black dot amidst deep green floated
as gingerly I returned the vessel to the high
shelf. The lack of clarity
around seeing and knowing what it was—
what was there—invoked
an ancient fear of God.

On the Road to Damascus

Traveling in a UN van I dreamed
of the days when that meant security.
Weighing the likelihood of a hijacking,
I regretted my desire to see John the Baptist's
head. My throat tightened as we bounced
along the newly-paved road (bad shocks).
I stared straight ahead to Damascus,
north of Amman. The Jordanian capital,
hotter than Hades, harbored the relative safety
of my in-laws. The driver stopped where
Eastern amenities lead Western travelers
to recall disciple Paul's rougher journey.
What am I doing, Lord, I whispered.

Looking over my shoulder, I spied
canvas bags tagged "Beirut." Diplomatic
pouches safer than any American.
Anticipating an explosion,
I prayed for safe passage.
A young Christian, I felt like a faux
VIP, acolyte of Joni's *hejira*.
Our children stayed with *Jiddo* and *Taytah*
as I made pilgrimage. I waited for a remote control
device to go off. I would be no martyr. My death,
a footnote. The press would be told that I went
to Damascus to shop in the *souk*.

A Bit of Mercy

In the ancient Imperial City of Meknès,
my guide, dressed in a black robe,
and surely too young to assume
such a posture, clasps his hands
behind his back, bows his head,
and strolls, under the narrow arched
passageways of the medina.

In Fès, the next day, I, consummate
consumer, enter a shop.
The shopkeeper's wife rolls up
the *djellaba*, sets the circle of folds
upon my American shoulders,
and the light wool fabric falls
like palms, just

before touching,
tempering the chill.
The robe grazes my ankles,
so my skin breathes. Years later
in New York at my desk, folds
gather in the crooks
of my elbows, nestling

against my thin skin.
Inside, I am restless.
A V-neck opening, lined
with chevron stitches,
graces my throat. The cob—
the hood which comes to a point
—rests on the nape of my neck.

Sleeves, sans cuffs, cover
the back of my hands.
My robe, a bit of mercy.

Dispatch from Beit Jala, near Bethlehem

Through the wall, my husband, our daughter, and I were driven.
I snapped a photo, hoping our taxi would not be stopped.
We'd come all the way from New York. Messages layered
the grey concrete slab: *God is No*—the rest wiped out.
A beginning besmirched, then *like a disease*. Beneath that
all comes round followed by something unreadable.
Then, *Be LOVE You're FREE. Call.* Yes, all in English,
interspersed with drawings of the stumps of trees.
Sandstone rubble lay at the foot of the wall. Then,
a small green strip and finally the wire—a barbed wire fence.

Abouna Issa, the old priest, welcomed us into his old home—
the home where he'd been born. Under an arched doorway,
he said to my husband, Hani, "Now that your father, George, has passed,
I'm your new Baba." And the two men's eyes glistened.
    Issa and George had been friends decades before in Baghdad
        when George was a publisher and Issa a pharmacist.
            Issa had found young Hani hiding under the bed afraid of
            the needle needed for immunization.
Abouna Issa's wife, Linda, took Petra to the slip of arbor
wedged in the narrow backyard where they picked *eskadenia*.
        Hani recalled the sweet tart yellow fruit as a boy
            when he visited his mother's family in a house up the hill.
Linda and Issa had left Baghdad quickly, taking nothing with
        them.
Abouna Issa said, "It's not so bad, the hours I now wait to cross
to Jerusalem. *Insha'Allah*."

Baptism
      Al-Maghtas المغطس

The vial of soil fits
the palm of my hand, fingers
embracing the solid—yet
giving—foggy plastic casing.
My thumb rests atop the tiny rough-cut
cross carved from a solitary
piece of olive wood.

The lid touches the pad of my index
finger, my *digitus medius* leans
on John. The label's image—
in which Jesus is baptized—
sits upon the soft flesh
of my thenar eminence.
Jesus' belly is full

with a prominent navel.
Rising over John's shoulder,
a cross rests, palm trees
at Jesus' side. I tighten my grip
and shake just once
for fear of pulverizing
the precious cache

further. I don't trust the seal.
I don't want it to seep
like the Holy Water
which evaporated
from the other
keepsake bottle.
Inside, a few terra cotta

chunks that would take a lifetime
of quaking to distill.
Not wanting to release
from my hold, I roll it gently
delighted by a soft click
like beads. But it quickly turns
into a faint rattling like bones.

Basilica Cistern

Medusa is turned
Upside down.
A second Medusa lies
Flat, like she is asleep.
The Turkish guide says Christians
During the Roman era
Were not quite ready
To let the ways of the pagans
Go; and no one knows for sure
Why one Medusa is topsy-turvy
While the other, sideways. Some say
Medusa gorgonized herself when she glanced
Askance. It seems to me,
A lapsed Methodist,
The Christians spooked
By Medusa sought to put her
To rest—upend
Her influence. Her power
Reigns aground.

Gadarene Rush

A campus courtyard in New York State makes me long for
Jerash, the still-inhabited Greco-Roman city, in Jordan.
The fountain, which flows in spring, is silent in winter.
At this moment, no one crosses it, nor lingers.
Students oblivious to the pastoral, rush
in the hermetically-sealed corridor.

The Jerash nymphaeum no longer flows.
Residents cross the colonnaded street,
to and from work, the madrasa, the souk.
A shepherd pauses with his flock to chat with US
tourists. The Jordanians joke the American presence
is so great, Jordan could be the 51st state.

I watch the students and wonder how many
know the architect of their campus,
renowned for his Islamic designs.

Snowomen

I stand, hear
in the US
northeast winter.

As one mindless win
after another blows
up Aleppo.

I lift a fallen birch bark
cast off from the neighbor
woman's tree crusted with snow.

The lenticels—pores
in the bark—strafe—a Russian
fleet of bombers.

Camp tents huddle
in shadow of glittering
pines. The miserly sound of the win, din

in the winter sum
does not resound
in my backyard.

Witless is the sound
droning air. I, listless,
listen in.

Fusion Approach to Gathering

                        At the appointed time
                        the fox appeared at the raven's house.
F^3EA:
Find—   The raven
                        flew up to a date palm and began
Fix—   to knock the finest and sweetest
                        dates down
Finish.   into a dense thorn
                        bush which grew below.
Then Exploit.   The raven invited the fox to eat his fill:
                        "Let none be abashed but the devil;
                        eat, brother, until
                        you can eat no more!"
Analyze   How eagerly the fox ran
                        round the bush
                        trying to pry out
                        at least one date!
through intelligence, surveillance, and reconnaissance.
Operators fixing the target—But the thorns were like needles,
                        and all he got for his pains are torn
                        paws. How enviously he watched
                        as the raven who
exploited the intelligence the raid yielded
                        snatched
                        date after date
turned raw data into usable knowledge.
                        from the spines
By doing this, speeded up the cycle
                        with his armored claws and strong beak.

Efflorescence

The tree in bloom takes the woman hostage,
drugging her with its colossal powder puff. Peaking

star magnolia tepals morph into bathroom tissue of a high
school unspooling. But it's too early in the spring for a lark

usually reserved for the coach's lot anyway.
Soon any trace of brilliance will vanish

and the woman will sink back into stacks of books
secured under the watchful eye of the PATRIOT

Act, buried in dust mites.
The petals flutter, surrendering

to Nature, despite a few that
cling as if hot glue gunned

after a dogged winter. Now the woman sees
scraps of bandages calling up wounds

of the earlier Desert Storm waged in our name
against people whose names we can't pronounce.

Streaming live public radio announces the Nagasaki
official's US trip, and before her very eyes

the tepals transform into paper cranes.
By turns, limp, the tepals invoke

the down of goose feathers. One rumpled past
bloom stands out, a dove. The woman searches

for more symbols of salvation. Instead,
the detritus of shredded paper

towels, remnants of cleaning rags,
crumpled pages, bone white teeth flood

her mind. While the blossoms on this perennial formed,
reports from Ramadi bombarded the home front.

She taps, "What flowers in Baghdad this week?" positions
the cursor, depresses the mouse. "Send Now," a missive

to the gap-toothed boy who mowed her lawn, off
fighting in Iraq. The flowers' heady fragrance slips

through a crack in the window, smacks of a wake, piercing
dust carried by April winds that permeates the air of her colonial.

She walks outside, picks a tepal and raises it to her lips.
For a moment, the woman, who scrubs fruit free

of pesticides, feels liberated and emboldened.
To the Iraqi people—not all of whom feel liberated

and only some of whom feel emboldened.
Then, the stench of industries west of her land

blows east, reminding her no chemical weapons were found.
Her face burns as Bush declares war upon the world.

The following morning she awakes to the rumbling
highway department contraption grinding brush.

She grabs the camera to capture any remaining flowers.
The tepals pale under cloud cover. Green buds assert

themselves. The woman stands beneath the canopy
and pinches the rubbery soft skin freshly fallen

from a branch. It is cool, damp, and surprisingly firm. Misshapen now, the tepals no longer resemble their nascent form

as they approached the pinnacle of their days.

Heavenly Bodies

This is the first full moon to fall
on the June solstice since the '67 Summer
of Love and the Arab-Israeli War.

Awakened by my beloved
from *rakı*-induced sleep,
the Fitbit on my wrist flashes 1:06.

I fall back to sleep and dream of the body. A dreamy
physician asks a technician if she thinks it's cancer.
In the nightmare, I wait, not breathing, thinking, it cannot be.

Waking at five, I unfurl my fists, and roll out of bed.
I thank god for trees—whose names I don't remember,
yet love just the same. Perhaps that makes me a lesser lover.

The blueberry muffin's tastier than yesterday's,
but the calories remain the same. I blame *Habibi*
for buying what he rarely eats.

I spend time with the dead and the comics.
None make me laugh nor cry. So I head upstairs
and go to work. I open the Arabic keyboard

to edit a document. Then,
in Instant Messages I type   Hani, What is the last letter in the Arabic
 word for "revolution"? I have sheen,

 wow, ray, & 1 more—
 maybe with two dots over it…?
 Does this look right, ثورة ?

I address   Homeland Security: This is not a call to action.
Hani's answer appears
                             First letter is *tha'* (as in theory)
                             not sheen. Last is *hamza maksura*,
                             circle with 2 dots on top.

                  Change first letter to *tha*
I make the correction. It goes like this all day, cleaning up
the manuscripts. Over lunch, the radio

reminds me it's the solstice. Daydreaming
lands me back in Stonehenge within the interlocking
sarsen circle where visitors can no longer stand.

Slim chance we'll return to the Sphinx, where the sun sets
between the Pyramids of Giza on the solstice.
I go back to edit "Savage Sausages."

The landline rings
                             Do we need anything?
                             Just you.

When Hani comes home, we drink wine
and talk about the war with ISIS. We hold
each other under the first full moon since '67 to fall

on the June solstice, as Earth—
at 23° 26'—reaches maximum
tilt toward the Sun.

Cue the Leaf Blower

Curse its drone—the air
In which it thrives. Curse the sidewalk
Blown free of twig and leaf and detritus,
Child and dog chased
Too. Curse the drone, air
Cursed where it flies. Drone on
Generals. Gnats. Drones.
Curse the domestic leaf blower.
May the fan housing blow, so
The air stream no longer aligns
With the handle. May stress on arm
And wrist multiply. Drone on. Curse
The drone. Curse the leaf
Blower. May the blowing tube length
Fail to adjust, forcing you to crouch
Squat, bend, and, ultimately, fall
To your knees. Curse the drone,
Air cursed where it flies—
Flies in the face of the accursed.
May your noise cancelling headphones
Lose charge. Curse the domestic
Leaf blower blowing. May the wind be
At your back. Accursed drone.
May carburetor and fuel system flood
With air. May the air come back to haunt
You with false starts and aborted
Missions. Sputter as hot chicks pass.
May your fuel tank leak.
May the sound pressure level
At your operator's ear climb
Beyond well beyond 92 decibels.
May your manufacturer warranty expire.
May the price of gas skyrocket.
May we rest in peace.

Endgame

I made good on my threat to leave home, if Ronnie became president;
and married Hani in Amman, where never was a proclaimed president.

We honeymooned in Egypt, where Sadat was an acclaimed president.
I snagged my heel, rushing to Hani at the casino, as if he was a famed
   president.

We sailed on the Nile in a felucca near the Valley of the Kings and
   Queens, where none buried were named president.
We've lived under one, then another, American inflamed president.

The dawn of the Arab spring deposed Mubarak, the shamed president.
We won't take our daughters to Egypt, under Sisi-nicknamed president.

Alexandria's Library awaits, for Hillary became not our dame president.
The lure of camel at the Sphinx is great, now that Donnie became
   endgame president.

Agora

The sound of water builds.
Water walls fall.
The sound: how one imagines
Two ginormous structures
Collapsing. A ginormous chorus
Voices thousands. Falls overlap,
Meeting, cornered. Sound nearly
Drowns living. Breeze in trees shade.
Water volume diminishes
As it falls into the base
Of the fountains' center squares.
The zephyr carries a drop
To one arm; then, another.
The drop—a single tear.
Our gaze falls upon a sea of names.
Behind our backs we hear the drone
Of a plane or something else
On the verge

Cross Border

Yolk of sun breaks as an incendiary inaugurates clouds of deregulated soot. Yolk of light runs energy above base overshadowed land. Fog shrouds lies. Lines ride into a black gathering storm. A million pink hats bloom: our sea of amber waves. Beloved mountain knows no boundaries of nation race gender religion; only its own: nature's notch on the horizon. Peaking obamian blues. Purple majesties. Beneath roiling yolk, power lines—short the Western staff—spark a new song.

Sun yolk tossed above cast iron skillet
Bursting flame on
People march march

Notes

Epigraph from *The Cathedral Builders: the Story of a Great Masonic Guild*, by Leader Scott, 1899.

Page 5—Inspired by Anselm Kiefer's walk-in installation, "A.E.I.O.U." This vowel sequence was used by Emperor Frederick III as a reference to his secretly planned imperialistic claims. "Austriae Est Imperare Orbi Universo." http://salzburgfoundation.at/walk-of-modern-art/anselm-kiefer-2002/

Page 6—Traditional samplers are made by hand with thread on fabric. The form of this digital sampler is partially dictated by the Arabic language, which is written from right-to-left. A document in two languages with opposing orientations (bidirectional text) results in a somewhat unconventional format.

Page 16—Al-Maghtas (in Arabic: المغطس), also known as Bethany Beyond the Jordan, a UNESCO World Heritage Site.

Page 20—After the poem, "The Snow Man," by Wallace Stevens.

Page 21—Sources: Stanley A. McChrystal, "It Takes a Network," *Foreign Policy* (March-April 2011), quoted in Jeremy Scahill, *Dirty Wars: The World is a Battlefield*, 2013, p. 145; and Inea Bushnaq, translated/edited, "The Hospitality of Abu L'Hssein," *Arab Folktales*, 1986.

Page 22—Efflorescence: the peak or fulfillment; a bursting forth, culmination, the point or time of greatest vigor; rapid flowering of a culture or civilization. Tepals are one of the divisions of a flower perianth, especially one that is not clearly differentiated into petals and sepals, as in lilies and tulips.

Page 26—Sarsen is the type of sandstone blocks found in Stonehenge.

Page 28—The presidents (in order of appearance): US—Ronald Reagan; Egypt—Anwar Sadat, Hosni Mubarak, Abdel-Fattah el-Sisi; US—Donald J. Trump. The poem is a pronghorn—a form invented by the poet as an American English variation of the *ghazal*.

Page 30—An ekphrastic poem inspired by a photograph by Mark W. O'Brien. See Acknowledgements.

Dawn Marar was a finalist for the 2017 Pablo Neruda Prize for Poetry and selected poems appear in *Nimrod International Journal of Prose and Poetry*. She was also a finalist in the 2016 *Orison Anthology* of Fiction & Poetry Awards, and winner of the 2016 Stephen A. DiBiase Poetry Prize. Her poetry has appeared in *Up the River, Tribute to Orpheus 2*, and as a finalist in a *Chautauqua Literary Journal* contest. Her creative nonfiction was nominated for a Pushcart Prize. She has published short stories and nonfiction.

A graduate of Skidmore College, Dawn earned a Master's degree from Columbia University. She worked with social justice and human rights groups as a planner and community organizer. Dawn has lived in Jordan and travels extensively. She and her husband, Hani, live in New York's Capital Region and have two daughters.

www.ingramcontent.com/pod-product-compliance
Lightning Source LLC
LaVergne TN
LVHW041600070426
835507LV00011B/1214